Teen Angst Mix Tape Vol.1

Copyright © 2020 Honey Cummings. All rights reserved.

4 Horsemen Publications, Inc.
1497 Main St. Suite 169
Dunedin, FL 34698
4horsemenpublications.com
info@4horsemenpublications.com

Cover by Battle Goddess Productions
Typesetting by Michelle Cline

All rights to the work within are reserved to the author and publisher. No part of this publication may be reproduced, stored in a retrieval system, or transmitted in any form or by any means, electronic, mechanical, photocopying, recording, scanning, or otherwise, except as permitted under Section 107 or 108 of the 1976 International Copyright Act, without prior written permission except in brief quotations embodied in critical articles and reviews. Please contact either the Publisher or Author to gain permission.

Library of Congress Control Number: 2021933894

Ebook ISBN: 978-1-64450-196-2

Print ISBN: 978-1-64450-197-9

Contents

Nia Maya Morgan............3

Miranda L. Scotti..........8

Brandon Mead..............16

J.M. Paquette.............20

Erika Lance...............34

Bre Brix..................46

S Rupsha Mitra............50

Oskar Leonard.............54

Valerie Willis............64

River Huckleberry Kero....72

Chrys Fey.................76

Paula Pivko...............82

Rae Harding...............88

Avra Kouffman.............92

Poems to Live By

Date: 2008-2011

The old me

Who you were then: During this time I was in 6th-10th grade, I was a small disabled black girl who didn't want to be noticed and was heavy into alternative rock (think, **GREENDAY**, **My Chemical Romance**, and Paramore). I wore a lot of black and spent a lot of my time in the library reading and daydreaming about what love looked like. As a young girl with Cerebral Palsy, I just wanted to fit in with my friends and I wanted guys to like me and didn't know how to do either. So instead I wrote a lot of poetry about how I was feeling. Every one of my crushes has a poem or series of poems at the time it was the only way I felt like I could communicate to them. I never sent any of them except one (not pictured in this submission) that I found ripped up in my English class.

The NEW me!

Who you are now: My love for poetry has never ceased. At 24, I graduated with my Master's in Creative Writing and I now work as a Tech Writer. I have long abandoned my angsty teenage poems for more refined activist poetry where I bring awareness to racial and social injustice as well as give a voice to the difficulties of having various physical and mental disabilities. I still write poems about my crushes and occasionally rock out to the Emo music of 2008, but I am way more sure of myself than I was as a teen. Throughout the years, poetry has given shape to my personality and character. It's allowed me to *express* and **explore** myself in a way that no other outlet has and I am so grateful for that.

Nia Maya Morgan

Pain Of Life

Dedicated To:
By Nia M. Morgan

1. Pain is like a knife stabbing you into the back and you as helpless as you are can do nothing but yell in agony.

   It's like a rock in the middle of the ocean getting hit on each side by rushing waves that go by.

10. It's like a human leech, who sucks out all of your joy, happiness, and life-long dreams.

   Pain is a contagious and
15. deadly thing, it's sucks out the good and enhances the evil.

   Pain is pain and that's all it is!

Toxic
Deadly
Substance
Danger!

february 10th, 2011

~~locksmith~~

you stole my heart before I
had time to lock it away,
erased my words
before they could even be
spoken
captured by your dazzling smile
am I so hesitant as to go
lengths to see it again.
a randsom, I would not pay for
the return of my heart, just as
long as your willing to chance our
fate.
is there such thing?
IAN... my heart beats, my lungs
breathe, my head screams
until at last my words have
been said.

— xoxo Shiloh

6 Teen Angst

Toxic Cycle

Date: November 23, 2000

Who you were then: Sixteen-year-old Miranda was a Young Adult novel protagonist in the making. The epitome of a late nineties, white, middle-class, teenage girl. A naïve daydreamer who was also totally NEUROTIC. I was Editor-in-chief of the school newspaper, member of the literary magazine club, and stock girl at the local bulk candy shop. I loved history, math made me cry, and I spent P.E. napping on the bleachers as often as possible. I was your typical hopeless romantic, with an emphasis on *hopeless*. My love life up until then consisted almost entirely of me getting friendzoned by my unrequited crushes. I was afraid to get too close anyway, assuming they'd quickly realize I was boring if they knew me too well. I lived in my own head, listening to LOUD PUNK MUSIC to drown out my thoughts and writing *angsty* poetry when that didn't suffice.

I longed to feel comfortable and accepted, but I was terrified of risks. Especially after one of my childhood best friends got hit by a car crossing the street late at night in ninth grade. She went into a coma that she never came out of and I became terrified that something bad would happen if I didn't follow the rules. I wasn't invited to many parties, and the ones I did tag-along to kicked my social anxiety into high gear. I'd either try too hard to act like I belonged, or completely shut down and hide in a corner where I could avoid socializing. But I couldn't ignore the *intrusive voice* in my head reminding me of *all* the things that could go wrong *all* the time. The perpetual worrying left me exhausted. I tried to be really thoughtful to make up for it so people would like me even though I was awkward.

My high school mantra was this: *it's easy to forget you're an outsider when people like you anyway.*

I could never pinpoint the origin of the unknown force that left me feeling like I was on the outskirts of my own life, observing instead of actually living it. Maybe it was my late summer birthday; I was always one of the youngest in my grade. Or maybe it was the constant thoughts swirling through my mind, demanding to be written down. Looking through my high school journals, *"Toxic Cycle"* is the poem that best encapsulates how I felt about myself throughout my tumultuous teen years. I didn't want to be just another girl who stood out or blended in too much. But I was a little too consumed trying to figure out who I was to ever actually find the answer.

The NEW me! Who you are now: Thirty-six-year-old Miranda is a Young Adult novel author in the making. The epitome of a pandemic-era, white, middle-class, mom. Truthfully, I'm not all that different than I was back then. I still have the same hobbies, quirks, and even the same best friend. The main difference is that I have names for all my ailments now. I understand that I was chronically worried because I have severe anxiety. I was diagnosed with OCD in college, and it was one of the biggest reliefs of my life to find out that there really was something chemically different about my brain that made me function the way I always had. I no longer look at it as something wrong with me, but as a part of myself that I'll always have to manage. It took until after college for me to also be diagnosed with chronic fatigue and a few other chronic pain syndromes as well. And seriously, if someone had explained to me that I was a categorical **introvert**, I think I would have been more accepting of myself and not have tried so hard to fight all my natural social instincts.

Even though I burned myself out on poetry and journalism during my high school years, my *dream* to be an author never faded away. It wasn't until I hit my thirties that I fell in love with contemporary YA romance and decided to start writing it. I probably spend way more time than the average person in their late thirties thinking about high school. How it's a time to screw up and analyze who you are but not quite get it yet. A time to **GROW** and **LEARN** about others in ways that may not make sense until you're older. A time to figure out all the stuff you do and don't want when you "**GROW UP**"–whatever that means. On one hand, if I could go back, I'd have a lot of wisdom I'd want to impart to young Miranda, like that she was anything but "just another stupid girl". On the other hand, I think it's better that it took time to learn it all. Now I have a really cute husband, two awesome kids, and my *dream job* at a library. It took time, but I guess you could say I eventually **broke the toxic cycle** and became everything I always wanted to be.

xoxo

12 Teen Angst

Nov 23

Toxic Cycle

When it all comes down
 I've become everything I never wanted to be
Another face in the crowd
 Another lonely heart
And just another stupid girl.
 I'd convinced myself I was different
 The smile on my face
 Laid in my heart as well
Until I saw the truth
 Buried in the lie that I created
And I realized I was just another name on the list
 Another face in the crowd
 Another lonely heart
And just another stupid girl.
You can use me
 And I'll pretend I don't care
Go ahead and ignore me
 But I'll still be there
Sitting alone on another afternoon
 Another name on the list
Another face in the crowd

Mix Tape Vol. 1 Toxic Cycle 13

Another lonely heart
And just another stupid girl.
I'm not the first to go down this path
Which makes it even worse
Because maybe I was ignorant
Or maybe things have changed
Maybe it's all imaginary
And I'll feel this all again on another day
Sitting alone again on another afternoon
Another name on the list
Another face in the crowd
Another lonely heart
Because it turns out —
I'm just another stupid girl.

DRIP

Date: 2001

The old me — Twenty years ago I was walking out of my homeroom class writing this poem. I had just turned fifteen and was very upset about a boy. He and I had shared something intimate, but in 2001 that wasn't a very cool thing to talk about in public. Especially not in high school when your "not-boyfriend" is known for being a tough guy. I wasn't hiding who I was as much as he had to, but at the time it hurt to feel ignored, even if it was for safety reasons in our small southern town. I envied my girlfriends who could express their feelings for boys without consequence and cried about that particular boy quite a bit. Hence the title of the poem I eventually made a collage from with magazine clippings and glitter: *"Drip."* The bedazzled version has since been lost through the course of multiple moves over two decades but the original, which I scribbled in all caps with Sharpie before gym class, has survived.

Now, I can barely remember that boy's face. I think we're friends on social media but I honestly have no idea. **The NEW me!** There have been many boys, and eventually men, since that poem was written. Most came paired with a decent amount of **heartache** but far more honesty. I'm happy to be living miles from that small town with my boyfriend in Seattle where I still write to sift through my feelings, but have a better handle on not giving my emotions to people who are not prepared to return them. I tend to compose most of the personal essays and fiction I publish on my phone, though I do sort of miss hastily scrawling bad poetry in permanent marker. There's definitely some **RAWNESS** we've lost since the days before we all had digital notepads in our pockets. One thing that hasn't changed: I still sign my initials the same way but with a more pronounced A in the middle. -BAM.

Mix Tape Vol. 1 Drip 17

Drip

It's suddenly a matter of connection
When different eyes stare back at mine.
Songs become sentimental again
And the old starts to fade away.
He hands me love that dies —
She listens with unknown power.
Life starts just as ~~break~~ slowly
When I know how much I want her.
I'm dreaming in the daytime
And wanting her life by night.
Envy shines in peaceful eyes
But his smile would never stop my tears.

Track 4
J.M. Paquette

Poems 1994-2002

Date: 1994-1998

The old me

Who you were then: These poems range from when I was 15 in 1994 to 19 in 1998 (though I added one from 2002 that is about that same time period). I was an *overly romantic*, **gullible** DREAMER who experienced a lot of life changes in a few short years--I had typical teenage drama boyfriends throughout high school, but the summer after graduation, my boyfriend committed suicide. I moved into my first apartment, got my first dog, and paid my first bills. I had a mostly fun job working in a comic book store (everyone wasn't like Padriac!), and I had to get a real job in an office while going to college. Luckily, the comic shop opened a new location, so I could work there enough hours to pay my bills (the 90s were so affordable where I lived!).

Who you are now: Now, I'm still a *dreamer*, but I'm also a writer, an editor, and a professor. I started working as a graduate assistant in the early 00s, so teaching undergraduate courses plus my hours at the comic book store got me through college. I eventually earned my PHD in English, and now I have tenure at a school that allows me to write fiction instead of academic research. Unearthing these old poems was an interesting trip down memory lane. I hadn't forgotten the people or the places or the faces, but re-reading these words brought me back there in the way only old journals can--like old photos of long dead relatives. You can just see the hint of resemblance in the CURVE OF A SMILE, the *shape of the eyes*--you know you're in there somewhere, and if you squint hard enough, you can see the person you used to be. And still are, in some ways.

The NEW me!

Temptation

lives in apartment 204
with soft curly red hair and inquisitive eyes,
a sunny outlook and a refreshing perspective.

Temptation know every want,
everything you think you need,
and offers willingly the things you would take for granted,

Temptation hears every little complaint and always sides with you,
learns the multiple meanings of every heated discussion and knows that you are right.

Temptation wants to satisfy you,
wants to show you new things,
wants to seduce your pristine thoughts toward sordid dark imaginings.

Temptation always leaves the door unlocked but has triple locks on the inside.

Temptation insists that no one will know,
that no one will see,
but you know what that really means.

Temptation will always offer that one thing just out of reach,
but once taken
becomes mundane,
transformed into what you had before.

(1997)

Crossing Signals

We needed some time to work out this strange
                         phase she's been going through. I ever knew why
he never really listens or learns; he just gets by. It's like he's looking at me
                         but she's always got her eye on some other life where
he tries to get it but he just doesn't see. I should have known
                         things would go down this way. She won't even let me keep my damn dog
that we're going to share. He demands His things but I think
                         that everything I paid for should get packed. What kind of person does she think
I am? He can have his stupid stuff if he wants. Except the bed—should I be forced to
                         survive without my possessions? And maybe it doesn't matter much
since he's being such an obstinate fool about the whole thing. Let him
                         sleep in a hotel for a few months until she works through the
end of our life together. It's time we moved on. We're finished
                         and maybe someday when I can afford to face her again I'll get the rest of my things.
We can't move the fish tank; besides, it was My Birthday Present
                         that she never really asked for or appreciated. The whole problem
is that we never quite clicked in a permanent way. He was always so
                         financially supportive while you went to school. And now that it's my turn
he will never learn. He will do nothing but hold me back. I'm better
                         than I because she works with Those People and I just cut sheet metal
wasting his time. He'll never be more than he was when we met
                         and everything was fun and exciting and promising a happy future
when someday life will be better and now that it is
                         she's found someone more promising than me. Drives a Mercedes;
a really nice guy. He listens and nods in all the right places
                         and He probably takes her out to the opera and races. I was never really
able to afford such a life. He's devoted his life to helping others, unlike some
                         who have worked every day since I was fifteen. Taking care of my mother
and he buys me nice things. I never thought life could be like this without
                         depending on my paycheck for details. I doubt she ever really changed from
what I was before. And he was always the same, and that's the whole problem
                         that she'll never be the girl I wanted her to be. She'll be the girl I once
knew and he'll never quite grasp the reason I needed to change.

(1997)

Note: I used to game (Dungeons and Dragons) with a group that included an older couple who had been high school sweethearts. She left him for a classmate when she finished college, and the break-up was messy. I never gamed with that group of people again. I stayed in touch with him—he eventually met another woman who appreciated him. They have a few kids and are happily married! (She moved away and I never spoke to her again.)

Untitled

Leaves in his shock of dark curls
Sunlight speckled across his smooth skin
Starlight sparkling in honey eyes

Knowing the other would be disappointed
Hoping the other would notice
Wishing for the other's frustrated silence

Yet all a cover blown free of casings
The Moment he drew near

The petty excuses
The ridiculous games
The burning thirsting need for revenge

Sated within an infinite universe
Of awesome potential
And wonderfully unknown pitfalls

And that was just the first time

(1996ish?)

Note: High school hijinks. Old boyfriend. New boyfriend. The usual.

Bob's Gravestone Gift

Bob wrote me a story once because he said I needed it.
It was about a girl who goes to a graveyard
to place lilies on the fresh grave of her dead lover,
written like a pure dose of Bob,
gritty with muddy feet and rain-splashed cheeks,
the damp dragging hem of a nightgown complete with faded blue lace at the neckline
and wrists.
A far cry from my own traditional t-shirt, but I guess that's how he saw me,
always with wet hair and in some clingy material.
Just like a man.
It had a real sense of place, you know?
Like I had been there the night before in my dreams, and Bob had been watching,
taking mad shorthand notes as behooves a real writer.
He said I need to get the guilt out of my system. To see myself going to his grave,
mourning him properly, then moving on, soiled dress and all.
I had told him, of course.
Close friends share all the nasty details: his last smile, the morning phone call,
going to his room one last time when Ducky let me in.
Talk about eerie.
And I told him about the patch of discolored carpet in her bedroom
I couldn't help noticing
as I collected the things I had left.
I admitted taking his favorite pen, his worn shirt, and my framed picture on his desk.
Silly, like the shorts at Chris's house, but still necessary.
"I'll call you once I know everything."
Barb's dazed shattered knowing voice on the phone
the last time I spoke to her.
And then there was the damn teddy bear.
"Barb took it," Ducky said, his once gleeful face creased by fatigue.
"She said he would want her to have it."
Yeah, in her dreams.
Still, how ridiculous to get worked up over a ball of fluff with a missing plastic eye,
knowing that, and yet still furious, ranting in Chris's room,
"Who the fuck does she think she is? What does she think she was to him?"
And his silence, big hands running helplessly through blonde hair leaving spikes of worry.
But he wanted ME to have it. Last week. He said.
I know. Come here.
(But you don't, do you?)
Never mind. It doesn't matter anyway.
It's not like I'll forget without the stupid bear as a reminder.
But it was his and I wanted it. Like the shorts.
Random items strewn across his friends.

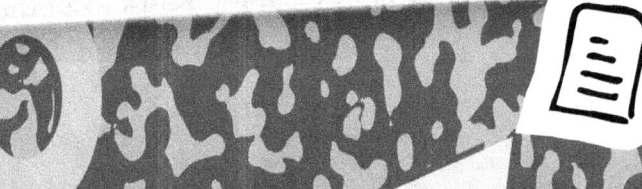

"You're not gonna get all weird on me, are you? They're just shorts."
Chris's face as he emptied the dryer, folding the purple plaid item in question,
peering at me with that palpable, damning concern
like he was waiting for me to shatter at his touch.
I couldn't call Ducky, I had told Bob. I couldn't ask him where he was buried.
I couldn't look at him after he handed me that box with the grisly surprise.
"He was wearing it at the time. I figured he'd want you to have it."
Gee, thanks.
(Why does everyone seem to know what you would want except me?)
So Chris and I waited for a different phone call that never came.
No funeral. Nothing.
That bitch always wanted him, and in the end, when no one could have him,
she kept him from us.
It wasn't real—too easy to think he was just away somewhere,
the empty space where he used to sit just waiting for him to reclaim it.
(And how long do my promises to you last?)
But the week turned into a month,
and the month into half a year,
and then Bob's face,
and his pen,
and his story of the girl who finally got the chance to say goodbye.
"He didn't have a gravestone for you. So I made one."

(1998)

Note: My boyfriend committed suicide when I was 18. His roommates didn't tell us where he was buried. To be fair, after that phone call from Barb, I didn't ask. A few months later, Bob wrote me a story and gave David a grave. It helped. I wrote this poem a year later.

Miss you

The Initial Issue

No one could quite remember the reason why
Necia looked so annoyed each time she walked by,
but Jean recalled a certain conversational moment
during which she might have received partial atonement,

while Shannon was convinced the whole situation just wasn't fine
since they always expected everyone to meet deadlines without overtime,
and Debra Ann spent all day long recounting the newest saga
of her latest cosmopolitan love interest who just waved sayonara.

Tara was in and out a lot, always had appointments
for dentist's drills or chiropractic skills involving smelly ointment.
Vivian was a palpable presence although she'd been fired,
echoes of her Southern drawl reverberating since she'd "retired,"

and Karen was hardly ever there, always on vacation
to other places with willing faces in homes across the nation.
So Corena played her eyes and ears reporting all she saw
of emails sent and gossip spent and cavorting in the hall.

Everyone smiled and nodded so nicely, pretending oh so well
that the problem had been rectified, the situation swell.
But attitudes and egos can't possibly manage to give in
when you've got a building filled with too much estrogen.

(1997)

Note: This was written after I got my first office job. I made it a few months, then escaped back to the comic book store when they opened a new location.

Padriac's Presents

The lull between morning and 2pm
between morning die hards and high school kids
finds me clinging to the crooked stool, checking out the latest *Nightwing*,
wondering if perhaps Bruce Wayne really did lose his shit and murder that girl,
what with all the evidence stacking up against him and even Dick Grayson starting to doubt,
when Padriac Glendenning arrives.

I don't look up as the door opens,
the stench hitting me across the room, and I know what I'll see—
Padriac in a sweat-stained t-shirt,
his white hairy gut rolled between the frayed ends of the shirt and the top of his sweatpants,
running those filthy slimy hands though the psoriasis chunks flaking to his shoulders
as he smiles at me through coke bottle lenses.

I want to feel bad for him, but I passed that stage a long time ago.

"Hello, Sweetie," he croons,
like being male gives him the right to call me that,
and I glance up from my book,
bored expression firmly entrenched,
knowing that the slightest hint of friendliness will condemn me.
Sliding carefully from my perch, I collect his books from behind the counter,
wishing my shirt covered the newly exposed skin on my lower back as I squat
since I can feel his eyes on the inked character of my tattoo.

I stand, laying the books down on the glass counter,
and his gaze travels down from my breasts to the bagged and boarded prizes of the day.
Pushing his glasses up his nose,
he is lost in the complete absorption of the true comic book junkie for a few blessed moments,
then he holds up *Transmetropolitan*. "Did you read this one yet?"

Now the quandary—
Do I say yes and hope that he drops it since he lacks the knowledge to comment
or say no and pray that he leaves it alone since neither can have anything to contribute?
No matter what I say, he will open the book
and waste ten minutes of my time pointing out great moments that I couldn't have noticed
because I'm just a girl
without any true appreciation for the fine nuances of story and artwork.

Taking the plunge, "Yeah," while trying to sound as preoccupied as possible,
careful study of Oracle's quirked eyebrows as she tapes up the ex-Robin's ribs again.
Padriac opens his mouth to speak in a cloud of reeking fumes,

but I catch him, "It was good."

He grins a little,
acne cheeks tightening as if we share some kind of secret across the counter.

I shudder inside.

"Is that it for you?" Maybe he learned to take hints in the last week?

No such luck;
he looks at the boxes labeled "18 and UP Only—This means you, John!"
and winks at me, "Anything new come out?"

I sigh, heaving the box off the shelf and plopping it on the counter.
"I don't know. Let me know when you're ready to go,"
and then I walk farther into the store,
away from the sweat smell and the greasy hands,
and begin studiously reorganizing Magic cards at the far end of the counter,
congratulating myself for a match well played.

Too soon he is lumbering over,
piggy hands clutching the newest *Bondage Fairies*,
looking positively gleeful about the image on the cover prominently displayed,
like I might be shocked by pornographic comics since,
after filing them for years,
I really never knew they existed.

"Do you have a bathroom in here?"
Oh, no.
No, but I can feel a bubble of laughter coming on at the thought,
and then I am speaking,
"Yeah, there's a customer bathroom in the back issue room."

"Can I use it?"
His face dares me to say no, but I just want him away from me,
so I answer, "Sure."
Then look away as he hustles the porno book into the customer bathroom,
waiting for the door to shut before I begin snorting with wild laughter,
praying that Scott comes in before close
willing to take one for the team
and brave whatever perils Padriac has left behind.

(2002)

Note: Yes, I know it's technically not TEEN angst, but this was the culmination of years working at the comic book store (aged 18-24). Padriac was not the only customer who did this, but he was the worst. (I was reading Nightwing #65; in case anyone is concerned—Bruce Wayne was totally innocent.)

Flagg

Barely surviving
      like Bilbo's lost buttons
he squeezes through the cracks

 like the insects and the rats
 Who always lurk here
      he reeks of the middle

of slippage and lost socks
of things in between
     he knows all the secrets
of places he should not have been

The stranger from elsewhere
     the new freak next door
the one who walks between worlds
     is really such a bore.

(1994ish)

Note: I wrote this down after finishing Stephen King's *The Stand* for the umpteenth time.

Best Buy

What's the word for the way you feel after watching the pimple faced bean pole with the cell phone and suitably saggy slacks who absently wheels out your brand new 27 inch TV and watches it slide
                in
                        slow
                                motion
                                        into a disheartening three hundred dollar crash, shrugging, "Well, that's what the Styrofoam's for," as he bends time and space to cram the massive box into the four door Nissan Sentra they assured you inside it would fit into with no problem?

(1997)

Note: First apartment. First TV of my very own.

Dog Days

Exactly how much time does she invest
in making certain every last item has been removed from the garbage can,
in nibbling every available corner
until no wood remains unmarked by her presence
and no paint or finish survives unscathed,
in teaching every vacant sock exactly who is in charge
until it becomes a mass of soggy cotton slobber indistinguishable from the rest of her toys,
before lying down to a well-earned rest
on the white couch
next to the fleece-covered dog bed
and relaxing from a hard day's work?

(1997)

Note: First apartment. First dog. First and last white couch. #Mistakesweremade

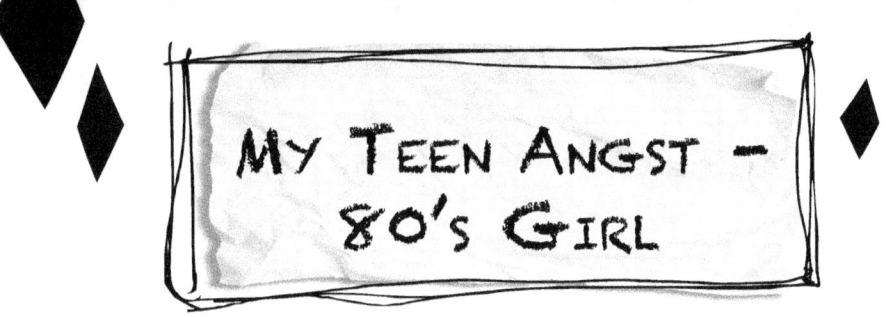

My Teen Angst – 80's Girl

Hello reader! Welcome to my teen angst.

A little about me, I was born in 1973. I grew up in **HOLLYWOOD CA**. When you get to know me, this makes a ton of sense and explains why I am the person that I am now.

This meant the main part of my teenage years was spent in the 80's which was a pretty rad dude! Like gag me with a spoon. Yes, I was a VALLEY GIRL for a brief time, which I am sure was annoying to many.

In case you were wondering... We did dress like this:

Well and like this:

Keep in mind, we did not have a "Hot Topic" store. We also did not have "MANIC PANIC" hair colors. If you were punk or alternative you had to actually work on it. I once put over 500 safety pins on a jean jacket. It was amazing, heavy and I couldn't wash it. It was fun being an outsider.

I also was sure to have a ton of NEON mesh shirts, jelly shoes and this iconic Madonna "BOY TOY" belt. At the time I had no idea what it meant.

This was the decade of music videos. **Video killed the radio star.** Of course it was back when MTV and VH1 actually played music. Vinyl records were a still a thing, my first was Broken Wings by MR. MR. We did not have CDs and instead walked around with Boom Boxes.

We were soooo hip!

Although, if you met me now, you would wonder how what I am about to explain could possibly be true. I was super shy growing up.

I was a nerd! In the 80's being a nerd was **not** cool. Not at all. I was the type of nerd that got pushed into lockers, never picked for team sports and basically ignored all through grade school and into high school. I spent most of my free time in the school library. It was safe there from you know bullies, since most did not care to read anything they were not required to.

If you are doubting any nerd cred, all you have to do know are the following three things:

1.) I saw **STAR WARS** opening night at the Chinese Mann theater in Hollywood. I was three and I wore a ladybug dress and my dad took me with a friend. It was amazing and the intro music still gives me CHILLS.

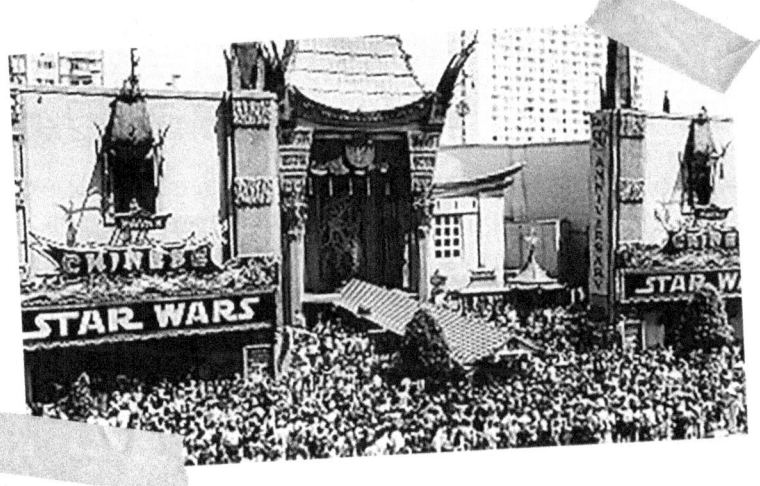

2.) I played **D&D** (Dungeons and when it came in a box set.

You actually had to use crayon to color in the numbers on the dice.

Imagine that fun. Now you can get *super fancy* dice made of a million different things, instead of hard ill balanced plastic.

Also, there was a point in time that the news started saying that those of us that played these games were all *satanic killers*. Imagine that fun.

Dungeons and Dragons: Road to occult?

When you told your parents you played a game and they feared you were joining a cult. I was lucky, my mom did not fear the "nerds". In fact, she embraced them. Which lead to me finding the renaissance fairs near where I lived and "my people".

3.) I read every *fantasy book* I could get my hands on. I could list them all here, but alas instead I am going to put a couple of my favorites.

I could fill this entire book could be filled with covers of the books I dived into, but that is not what this is for.

The last few pieces of the puzzle you need to know before you read my amazing poetry is that I *loved* Lisa Frank. Garfield was my favorite comic and I desperately wanted to have a boy romance me the way they did in every John Hughs movie. I wanted my own person like Jake Ryan waiting for me where I least expected it. Of course, who didn't want Jake?

Of course I never ended up having a Jake Ryan waiting for me outside a church where my sister was getting married, but I did find my prince charming, but that is a story for another time.

So, I began to write, starting with poetry and short stories. I also began to draw and paint. Mostly eyes at first. I am sure someone could tell me that meant something significant. If it did, I never caught on. So, enjoy my early teen poetry in its original form along with one of those **epic** eye drawings.

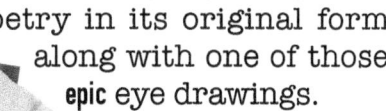

I will not hide, I will not flaunt.

I will not judge by actions.

This is my message to all that will hear.

~~Puttphph iiiihhh ihhphht~~

To breed life, to breed art.

~~I is~~ tis to smother prejudice ~~and~~ and drowned contempt. Would show a greater understanding of the Human Race.

Could you still see
the person in me as who
I am.
If sex is my body
and want is my soul.

Then ignorance is holy
and hatred a well.

To see any human
as an act, or lust.
is to put on blindfolds
~~and in a group~~

~~Would make us see~~
~~only the bad in~~

is to see any being
~~tread to a cage.~~ as
a blind man to a rainbow
~~Its~~ I told you ~~out~~
I was different out
of love not fear.

~~Shame is low.~~
Respect me not my acts.
~~Admiration is high.~~
~~for them you w~~
I know you are my
blight.

Mix Tape Vol. 1 My Teen Angst - 80's Girl

If I told you I was
differnt, what would
you say?

Would you shun me,
or hate me,
or push me away?

If I told you I was
differnt what would
you do?

Would you hurt me?
or leave me?
or want me to leave you?

If I ~~told~~ show you that I'm
differnt what could
you see?

Would it be a freak,
a disease
some kind of deformity?

If ~~I~~ ~~knew~~ you knew I
was differnt,

could we still be
friends?

42 Teen Angst

It began in the clouds.
At first it was new, moist.
It could feel the water.

It built itself.
I could feel it swell.
It expanded till it encompassed all is surrounded.

For a moment in time it held itself there.
Perfectly still.
It need not move for it knew its path well,
Then as the stars aligned,
And the wind kissed each side.
It felt the warmth of a sun play across it,

It began to desire the release,
It had grown to heights it did not know were possible
It wanted to share

Then it began,
Lightly at first, careful,
It remembered the pain,
It remembered the safety in being small,
This was frightening to it.
This was new.

Then when it realized that what it shared others wanted,
I yearned for it,
I needed it,
I drank it, and it filled me as nothing had.

It realized its power and gave more of itself,
It grew again,
It was larger then ones eye could see,
It held power,
It needed only itself now to know its strengths.

I watched this,
I was there, I thought,
I still held myself there taking all it was willing to give me,
Cherishing every piece,
I felt whole.

It began to grow again......

BELLY DANCER

"This poem is presented in all it's mediocre glory. It has survived two 100 years floods, one 500 year flood, a fire, a break-in, and nine moves. And it remains the most melodramatic angst I have ever penned."

THEN:
Bre Brix's mother often referred to her **EMO STAGE** as the Dirty Harry stage of her life. This dark-colors-only drama-club-member, poetry-writing, bad-boy-dating snowflake of a teenage was like so many others at the time. After a nasty breakup to fuel the creative fire she wrote a slew of dark poems attempting to capture the greater mystery of *angst*.

The old me

The NEW me!

NOW:
She was formerly a bead catcher from Mardi Gras Land and has rather ironically settled in the Florida Man Territory. Despite her melodramatic youth she has found her present to be bright working in the publishing industry avoiding the *belly dancing* career altogether.

Belly Dancing in Florida

I'm belly dancing in Florida
How grand it used to be
with all the attention, center stage,
I enjoyed the life I made
And I was belly dancing in Florida
the night I realized you weren't the one
the night we fought and words were said
that never found their home
and even when we parted
from the perfect three to none
I was still moving to the music
determined to go on
And I was belly dancing in Florida
When I realized where I was
and that all the attention was nothing
and my life was not my own
And the music lost its rhythm
and the words lost their rhyme
when I was belly dancing in Florida
wishing it was for the last time
But here I am still
promises come and gone
with all the same memories
and all the familiar songs
And I'm tired of dancing in Florida
and I'm tired of what I've become
but I wonder still what I would do
since this is all I've ever done.

Track 7
S. Rupsha Mitra

Untitled

The old me — Who you were then: I was a teen as I am now, however the poems were written specifically in response to certain events which evoked certain **INTRUSIVE** and *discomforting* thoughts in me and I discovered the best way to confide my feelings was to write them on paper and that is how the poems happened.

The NEW me! — Who you are now: It's just that I feel lighter, whenever a negative thought or anger casts over me, I write, lots and lots of poetry. It actually is so transformative - the anger can be transmuted into art which you can relish forever.

To a friend who thinks I am unnecessarily emotional

I know - I am a novice in

Trying to keep myself '' detached ''

I unfurl untimed

like an incarnadined sea whirling in emotions,

How I yearn for the soft hibiscus touch of mulmul breath,

how I disregard your logic of certainty and dealing with the self

like the heartlessness of stone,

how I yearn still to wet in the rain and feel

the aftertaste of rancid memoirs and

Grimy silts of gutters filled with embarrassing images of the past.

You might think I am crazy to be the way I am –

an incorrigible worshipper of nostalgia and bones – wintry and dried wisdom –

all that is left when the slushy heart grows old with the weight of

dampness. But I tell you, I am learning still,

the nuts and bolts of the nonchalant act of bolting,

locking the doors,

turning over the pages of an old album and walking forth

against parallax like sprinting trees –

this is difficult for me friend – this so simple act of letting go.

Now I accidentally mumbled something in my head that I should not have said

It's right we can't remember when it struck us,

a largesse of desire

dank, deodorised

maybe fluttering butterflies in our stomach

or hopeful angels singing against our palpitating breath and

an effortless epicurean moment evanescently fleeting by. We do not know where our roads would lead to , maybe we are

meaninglessly confused of our momentous revelry.

And disappointed with the terrible disbelief in love at first sight.

Maybe I am right it's not love.

And so must you be – as there's nothing special, no fate figured or divine destiny.

Its just time passing by captured like a photograph from

our crooked feelings and amorous smiles, upholding the unending conversation between our springscape skies.

Its just a thought, probably, of unrelenting longing,

or an abrupt emergence from the sulky mementos of past,

maybe a chalky firmament of wintrous dawn or

a faint glimpse refracting through our eyes.

An *excuse me* spelt even on an abandoned staircase,

an unknown goodbye.

A frisson so charming in the aura of dreamy twilight.

And today I suddenly thought of you. And suddenly said I love you..

Taking your stranger name to satiate the hungering nerves of mine.

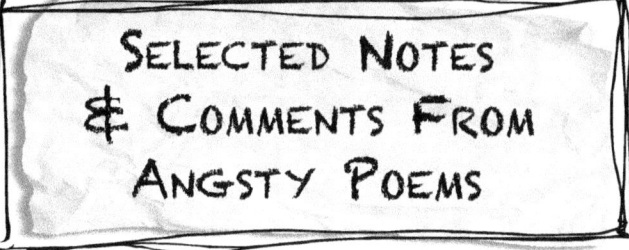

Selected Notes & Comments From Angsty Poems

Date: Circa. 2017-18

The old me

Who you were then: I was heavily *depressed* and swinging between brief HAPPINESS and horrific SADNESS. I hated everyone and loved everyone. I was tearing my family apart. I was **confused**. Some days, I wanted to end my life--others, I wanted to smile until my lips ached. Life threw me from event to event without a care. Anyone watching must've thought I was a mess. A *chaotic mess*.

Who you are now: I'm a lot more **stable** now. I have a good relationship, a better home life and much better mental health. I feel in **control**. I've been publishing my work, writing a lot more and focusing on the good elements of life. Not everything is sunshine and RAINBOWS, but it's easier to face **thunderclouds** with memories of sunlight.

Website: https://oskarleonard.wordpress.com
Instagram: @ozzywrites
Twitter: @leonard_oskar

Selected Notes And Comments From Angsty Poems

I.

it's short but yeah

hey it rhymes

that's a first

II.

whoops

it's a bit dark

oh well

more rhyming

what's wrong with me

III.

yay

no more rhyming

and still depressing

woot

IV.

heheh

have you noticed yet?

comment

OOF ANGSTY

V.

whoops

a lil bit sad

haha

nevermind

at least it didn't rhyme

i don't think so

anyway

VI.

idk

i feel

complicated

(aka

shitty

aha)

VII.

oof

i feel

weird

idk

comment

This is so beautiful, and probably my favorite poem of yours so far.. I really hope you never stop writing poetry

ESCAPE

VIII.

(why

am i

even

still

here)

IX.

(meh

idk

what is this?)

comment

This. Is. POETRY.

X.

(i'm so

`freaking nervous

and i

don't know why.

this shit

is literally how i

feel right now)

XI.

(i'm pretty sure

you have no idea

what this is

about

and that

makes me

somewhat happy

you will

never

know

haha)

comment

oof

XII.

(hm

not too sure

about this

it's not

like

what i usually

write)

XIII.

(ah

idk

nothing i write

feels nice anymore

it all feels

weird

and cold)

XIV.

(mm

edgy stuff

but

whatevers)

XV.

` (ugh

life can just

go die in a hole

i'm so done

with everything)

XVI.

(fuck

everything

i hate

everyone

and everything

mostly everyone

ugh

life

sucks

so

fucking

much)

XVII.

(i

i seriously don't know.

whatever.

what's the point.

idk.)

XVIII.

(idk)

XIX.

(i'm so tired

so

so

so

so tired)

XX.

(i

don't

know

how

i

feel)

XXI.

(what

is this

feeling)

XXII.

(is this

happiness

or just

not being sad

idk

by this point)

XXIII.

(i wasn't dead

just

sleeping)

XXIV.

(it's

not a bad day

just

a bad life)

XXV.

(fuck

everything

and everyone

ever)

Track 9
Valerie Willis

Journals from Middle Grade through College

Date or Year of Teen Angst Moment: 1990's - Middle School

ITEM: Notebook passed between friends disguised as English notebook.

The old me

Who you were at the time it was written. What was happening in your life?
I was the quiet **awkward** one who drew pictures really well. My best friend at the time was super popular, but regardless, we were in our PRIME of wanting to know all the things about boys. From talking about our crushes and code-named them based on their initials combined with things we know they liked? I think that was the formula? COMICS, funny **AOL chatroom** crushes, and so much more unfolded though I never dated anyone. In fact, I am pretty sure we never dated any of the boys we talked about in these.

The NEW me!

Who you are now! Where has life taken you?
I AM AN AUTHOR! Telling stories, speaking at events, and designing books is my *dream job*, and now my day job. It wasn't a straight path, but compared to the **drama** of my past, life is much WILDER.

What color should I paint my Whats your fav. kind of nail circle 1!

← smell this 1!

smells → like chaclet

← Bluberey Smell

I don't know to choose? well I will go with this 1. ←

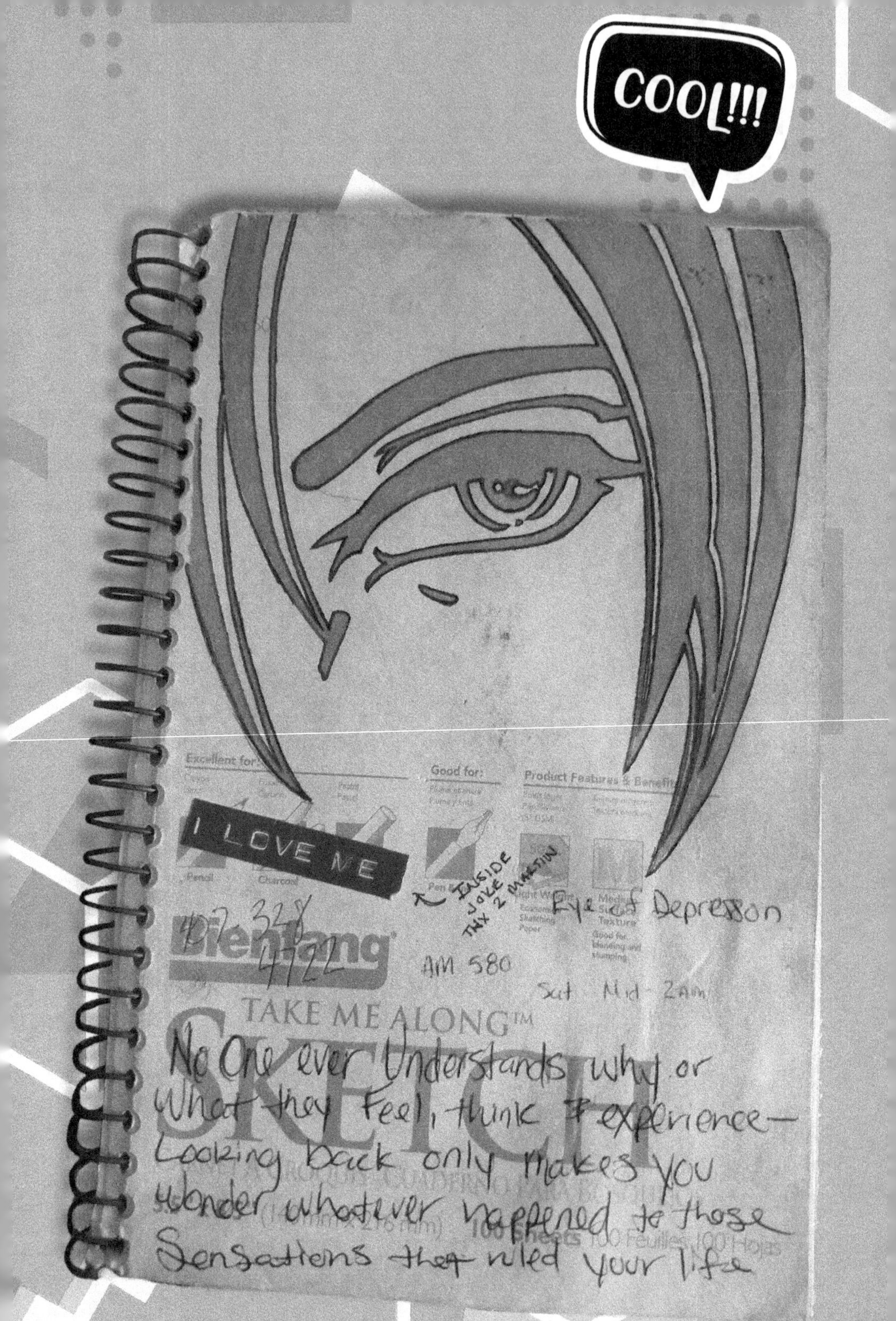

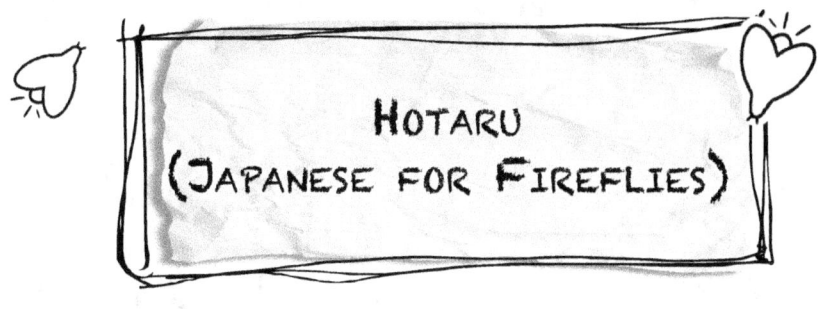

HOTARU
(JAPANESE FOR FIREFLIES)

Date: June 7, 2015

Who you were then: From April to August of 2015, I was on student exchange in Japan. At the time, I lived in Bella Bella, which is a small town on the Northwest Coast of British Columbia. Part of my dad's family is from Japan, so it had always been a *dream* of mine to travel there and when I was sixteen, I finally got the chance to!

The culture shock was immense and I learned some key things about myself. I learned a lot about my gender, my **independence**, and my mental health. I made some mistakes and I do still have my regrets from my stay in Japan (I wasn't as adventurous as I wish I was), but I kept a blog on WordPress the whole time that I was there. Of the fifty or so entries I made over six months, this one is my favourite.

Who you are now: The number one takeaway that I still have from this trip even though it's been five years (only five years?) is the lesson of *authenticity* and being **unapologetic**. I was very restricted in who I was while I lived in Japan, partly because of the culture and partly because of who I was at the time. Nowadays, I have reinvented my gender, given myself a new name, and **GROWN** as an artist and a writer. The things that used to scare me no longer do. I have new fears, now.

Since the trip, I have graduated from high school and I got my BFA. I have fallen in and out of *love*. I have **GROWN** immensely. Looking back at who I was then... I think I would have been *happy* to see where I am, now.

http://riverkero.com/
https://www.instagram.com/huckleberry.comics/

I had taiko class yesterday. I'm really starting to get the hang of it. But that's not the important part.

During taiko, I heard some of the kids mention "hotaru". I had no idea what it was, but I just sort of nodded along for a while and pretended that I knew what they were talking about. Until the translator person I was with came in and asked me if I'd like to go see the fireflies with some of the kids.

Oh.

YES. DEFINITELY.

I didn't sound super enthusiastic, though. I chalk that up to being tired from practice, then I realized what we were gonna do. *Fireflies.* I'd never seen them, before.

So we got into the car and drove across the river, to this little creek set into a concrete canal, one side of it lined with bamboo. The creek was full of tall reeds, and there were a few people wandering around as the sun set behind the mountains. The air was cool and clear, and it smelled so fresh. The sound of traffic was drowned out by noisy crickets and frogs. Moths hummed through the air, and clouds of gnats swarmed, then dissipated as the sky deepened from royal blue, to indigo, to black. We walked around and took a few pictures, but when I realized it was too dark to take good pictures, I put my phone away and didn't take it out again.

We stood in the twilight, eyes straining for a flicker. Once or twice I confused car headlights in the distance for a flash of firefly light, but that was mostly due to the fact that I wasn't sure what to look for. I also became conscious that I was pretty chilled, and started to rub my arms for warmth, not wanting to complain. I'm Canadian, after all. The cold shouldn't bother me.

Then we saw it. On a bamboo leaf, there was a little white pulse. It pulsed again, and again. We crowded around it, and the people I was with immediately started taking pictures of it. Naturally, after the first appeared, so did more. As I watched, more and more little pulsing lights began to appear. If you looked carefully, you could see them through the dense bamboo, up high on the leaves, or drifting lazily through the air.

We didn't stay much longer after that. I remember watching one girl, who looked about twelve years old or so, follow after a firefly with her hands held out like she was cupping rainwater. It looked very picturesque. She would make a good drawing, sometime.

We turned and left, after that. It was dark as we walked down the gravel path back to the cars, passing other families who were going to see the fireflies, and ducking under low-hanging bamboo leaves. A moth drifted lazily by, and I lifted a finger, touching its tiny feet as it flew off into the twilight sky.

It doesn't bother me that I never got a good picture of the fireflies. Some things are better left as memories.

Teen Crash Down

Date: 2009

The old me

Who you were then: I was nineteen when I wrote this poem to my past self, who had gone through a lot up to that moment in time. I looked back at every hardship I had faced, from **spine surgery** at fifteen to having to drop out of high school at sixteen and experiencing **domestic/sibling abuse** that was strongest and SCARIEST when I was seventeen. I'd gone through a lot. During those years, I felt so beaten down. I experienced my first bout of *depression*, couldn't see into the future, didn't know where my life was going, or what would be in store for me next. Most days, it felt as though I was the eye of a hurricane. **TRAPPED.**

The NEW me!

Who you are now: I have *grown* from all of those hardships. Each one made me **stronger** and WISER. Now, I am a published author with a 5-book (and growing) series under my belt, which blends a unique concept of disasters, crimes, and romance. I am an editor for freelance clients, as well as for a small publisher. I am following my *dreams* and will only continue to go further.

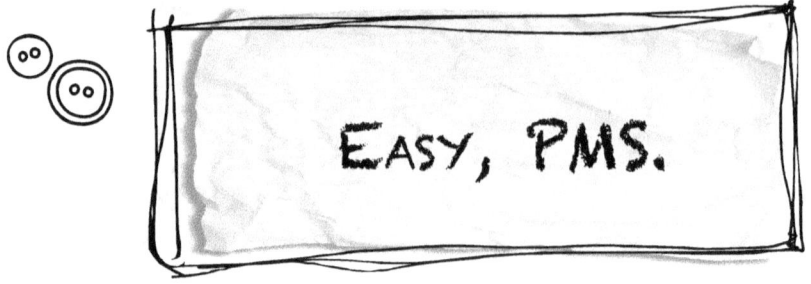

EASY, PMS.

Date: 2006

Who you were then: This is a snippet from a book I was writing when I was sixteen and in the beginning of eleventh grade, just before I had to drop out. I was going through a tough time at home. School was the only place I experienced any relief, but I also didn't want to be there for several reasons. I **COPED** by writing a young adult story, where the main character was myself, but she got to say and do things I never had the **courage** to do.

The old me

The NEW me!

Who you are now: I am a published author with a 5-book (and growing) series under my belt, which blends a unique concept of disasters, crimes, and romance. I am an editor for freelance clients, as well as for a small publisher. I am following my *dreams* and will only continue to go further.

Website: https://chrysfey.com/
Blog: htttps://www.writewithfey.com/
Bookbub: https://www.bookbub.com/profile/chrys-fey
Instagram: https://www.instagram.com/chrysfey

Teen Crash Down

by Chrys Fey

If I told you what would happen,
you wouldn't believe me,
you'd think I was deceiving,
sweet thirteen-year-old me,
it's happening.

When you're fifteen you'll go through a lot of pain,
but through heavy tears you'll continue to breathe,
nothing will stop you from healing from surgery,
and the scar soon won't mean a thing.

So don't look now,
it's the time of your life when your world comes crashing down.

When you're sixteen it won't be so sweet,
although you had to drop out you'll continue to dream,
nothing will stop you from becoming the best that you can be,
and the diploma you don't have will make you strive for everything.

So don't look now,
it's the time of your life when your world comes crashing down.

When your seventeen life gets really mean,
you'll never know where your bed will be,
or when your brother will start to swing,
but I swear you'll be okay!

So don't look now,
it's the time of your life when your world comes crashing down.

When you're eighteen you feel left out,
put down and kicked around,
forgotten by everyone you ever loved,
but I swear you'll find your place soon enough!

Sweet thirteen-year-old me,
you don't believe me,
you think I'm deceiving,
just remember to be me,
because I'm who you turn out to be.

Easy, PMS

By Chrys Fey

"My name's not baby cakes!"

"Whoa. Easy, PMS."

"For the first time, you've said something right. I am PMSing, and if you have a problem with it, then never get married!" I opened my purse, took out a tampon, and chucked it at him. "How's that for PMSing?"

The girls broke out in applause while the guys laughed their heads off.

MASKS

Date: approximately, 1980

Who you were then: In 1980 I was starting high school and felt pretty much **ALONE**. I think I had just lost my best childhood friend. One had become more interested in boys than me. I had others of course but they felt **super-ficial**. And I was shy. I was, and still am, the one at the snack table or against the wall at a party. The boys that were interested in me I saw as dumb and immature. If there was a boy I liked I wasn't going to ask him out, that wasn't my way. It just seemed like everyone was interested in being part of a clique that I couldn't be in. Normal teenage stuff I suppose. At some point in high school I saw a picture of a painting in a book. I can just remember, it was so long ago. I believe it was a painting of the artist surrounded by a wall of *masks* that filled the canvas. So from that I wrote *Masks*. Apparently judging from the poem I was trying to make myself feel better by saying I was genuine. I assume I was no better or worse than anyone as far as that goes. Anyway, entered the poem in, I believe, a state-wide contest. It got honorable mention and I went to a workshop in Jacksonville Florida. I wore my favorite dress for the last time as I had grown. I remember how tight it was. I tried to apply everyone's suggestions to the poem. For example, removing the ending, changing the rhythm. Never was able to do any better than the original so here it is. I kept writing and still do, off and on. Only now it's more on than off.

Who you are now: I went to college in Gainesville, Florida, and then in Miami. Eventually I graduated with a degree in Prosthetics and Orthotics. I worked in New Jersey for a while then returned to Florida and continued my career, first working for the VAMC and then for private artificial limb companies. Got married and divorced in 2008. I live in Port Saint Lucie Fl. I have two sons, one in college and one will graduate in 2021. About a year ago I joined a writer's group and began writing short stories. They've been published on Reedsy. I've also had some of my poetry published in the Florida Writer's Magazine. One of my poems was a finalist in the 2020 Florida Writer's Association RPLA awards. Currently I am work ing on a science fiction novella I hope to publish eventually.

Masks
By Paula Pivko
Year, 1980
Paulamartinek378@gmail.com

Everyone is a mask.
A cool and impersonal mask,
A mask with no soul.
A mask with no compassion.
A mask with no personality
A mask with no feeling.
Every mask is different
Yet, are all the same—
Alike.
Exactly like each other.
And you can make a mask.
The way to make a mask
Is very simple.
First you have to make a mold.
Start by shaping yourself
Into someone,
Someone,
Anyone.
Your best friend
Or your favorite movie star.
You mold yourself exactly like them,
It takes a while for it to harden.
Then—
You decorate the mask
By hiding yourself well.
That takes a while.
Then-
You put on the finishing touches
By hiding your feelings.
There!
You have a perfect mask,
A beautiful mask,
Cool and impersonal.
The problem with the masks is that
Once you have finished a mask
It's very hard,
Very hard indeed,
To break open
These masks.
It's hard to break open,
To get out and grow.

Because these masks
Are
Virtually
Indestructible.
But people never learn.
They make themselves into masks,
Thinking they can get out,
But they can't.
They are stuck.
No one weeps for mankind anymore.
But
Since I am no mask
I'll take up the job.
You can trust me.
I will never make a mask.
Let me.
Trust me.
Trust me, let me.
If you let me
I will weep
For all mankind
And all womenkind
And all childrenkind
In short
I will weep for everyone.

STUCK

ALTERNATE

Date: 1993-1997

The old me

Who you were then: This piece was inspired by a high school crush, an older boy, who already had a girlfriend, but had become, at that time, my best friend. Our friendship lasted on and off well into college, where we dated briefly over a summer. After, there was a decisive break from my innocent *teenage angst* to my cognizance of self-worth. Our relationship taught me the ills of *fantasy* and the ugly truth of *infatuation* when giving over one's self to another and failing to act on the potential we have hidden within ourselves that makes us **precious** and **priceless**.

The NEW me!

Who you are now: After a twenty-year career in the theatre industry, I am now a writer mom, homeschooling two children while wrangling a toddler. My husband and I have been married for eighteen years and foster parents for the past four. A NIGHT OWL since childhood, you can find me tapping away on my laptop sometime well past the midnight hour, working out dark *fantasy* tales of angels, demons, ghosts, and other paranormal entities. And the humans who cross their paths.

Alternate

There was a boy
who hid behind her to escape another.
She loved him instantly.

He lent her his jacket once.
It smelled like cologne
only a teenage boy would wear.

He played the drums
And her heart,
Taught her Kierkegaard,
and Jane's Addiction.
She confessed everything
except her love for Orion.

They steamed windows in a car
when he came home from college.
She was an other,
desperate
to make a blind boy
see his potential
and hers.

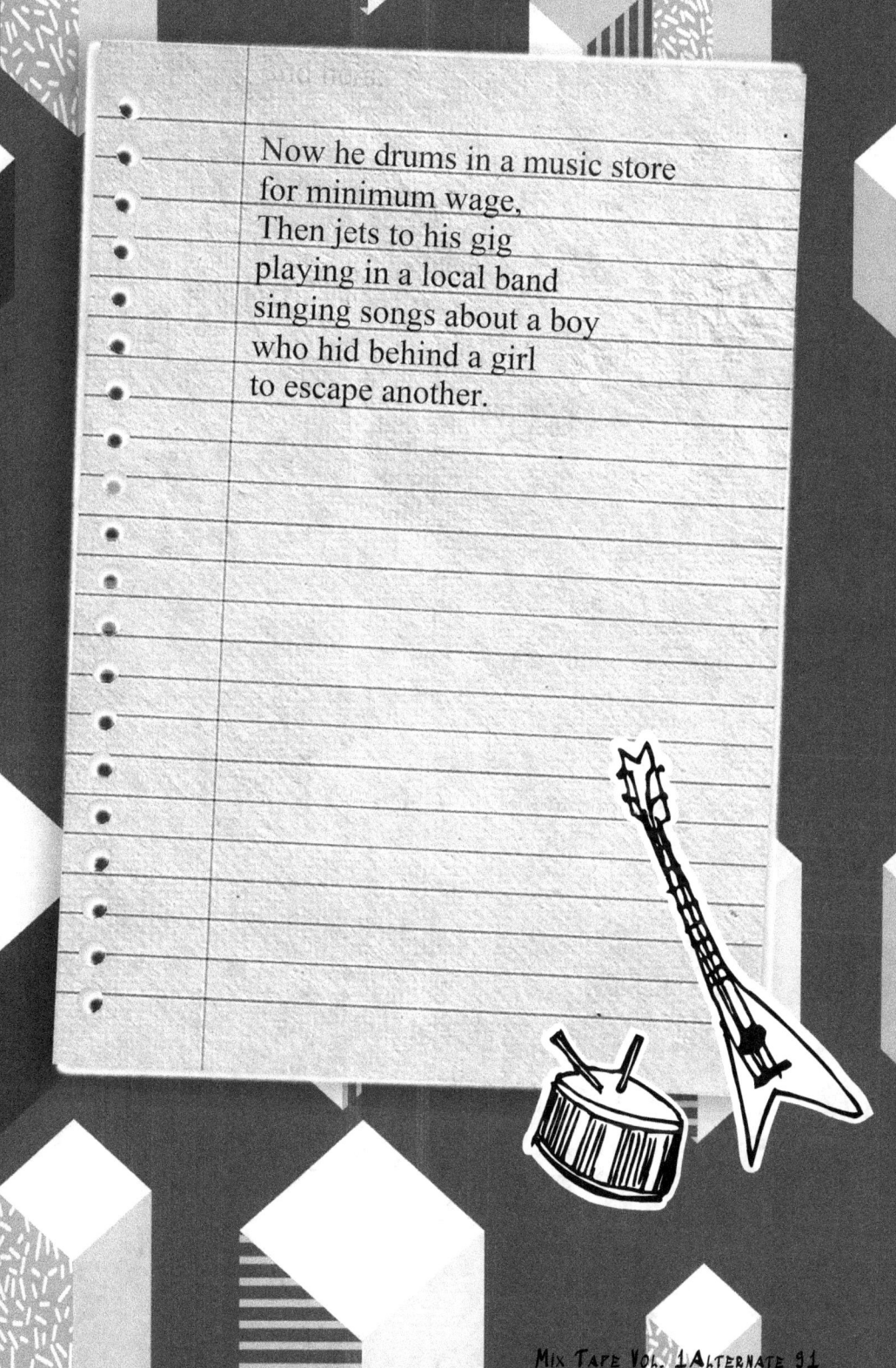

Now he drums in a music store
for minimum wage,
Then jets to his gig
playing in a local band
singing songs about a boy
who hid behind a girl
to escape another.

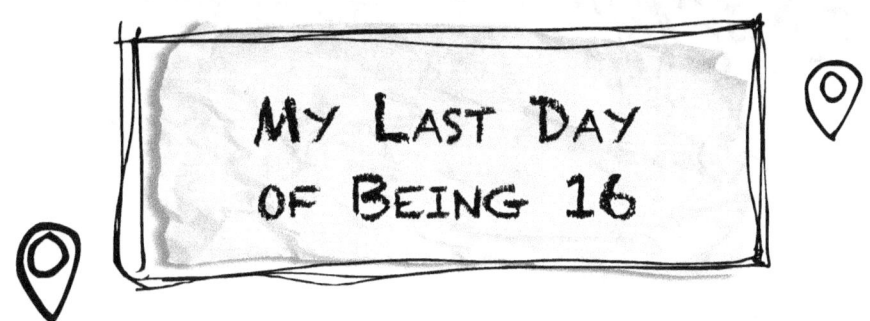

My Last Day of Being 16

Date: March 26, 1984

Who you were then: I was a **MUSIC**-obsessed, **TRAVEL**-obsessed, **magazine**-loving teen. I lived in Manhattan, New York City in the '80s, when the age to get into clubs was 18. The fake i.d. was rampant and venues routinely let in girls aged 15 and up. I spent countless nights seeing the **Toasters**, Rockats, Connotations, NED SUBLETTE, and other local bands. Many groups came over from London, too, and played The Ritz, the Peppermint Lounge, Danceteria and CBGBs. I loved that era.

The old me

Who you are now: I'm still a **MUSIC**-obsessed, **TRAVEL**-happy occasional journalist. Since 2005, I've lived in southern California. Prior to that, I lived in London and NY, along with stints in Moldova and Brazil. To this day, I quirk out on music and lyrics. Though I listen to songs from the early 1900s to the present, I'll always love the music of the '80s.

The NEW me!

Duran stands for "Duran Duran" and Smutty was Smutty Smiff, the stand-up bassist in the Rockats :)

Dear God, Thank you for giving me sixteen. I'm going to make something of seventeen.
Thank you
AVRA

Today is my last day of being 16. It's a nice age, it fits me, and I don't want to leave it. I will miss it more than some of my friends whom I will never see again.

I can't believe it - 17 - double that + it will almost be time for a midlife crisis. I like being young and new and everything being young and new. Happily though I feel almost safer and more relieved now though; as if 17 is a liscence to have all the adventures I want and do whatever I want to do. Because sixteen is the age to be sweet + pure - + I made it through at least sort of IN that condition!!

And I did a lot of the things you're supposed to do at sixteen: I had a beautiful boyfriend ♥Paul♥ if it was only 2 weeks and chaste so much the better (though I didn't think so then!) but I spent a lot of sixteen in the 130's - a happy place! 135 & under is, anyway. I remember really not being happy on my sixteenth birthday;

I didn't feel pretty enough to be up to it and my friends were being abusive to me - but I did make a lot happen this year.

I had many more boys interested in me, I looked much better, I felt better, I was accepted to real good colleges, I found the Alarm

– the best find since DURAN, SMUTTY is now aware of my presence + existance he seemed to like me! and on and on; oh also much better relationships with Em + Julie, AND FUN Club Nights – Billy Idol sigh.

I think the best way really to get over not being sixteen is thinking about all the possibilities and new avenues open to 17 (sexy + ...); I can use my feeling about what applies to seventeen as opposed to sixteen to my benefit. I'm going to think what I want now + then fulfill goals, or at least progress towards them (the road of life how corny) like CRAZY!

april   EXCERCISE! – please it's good for you, clears your head, gives you nice thighs for fun bikini + clothing action

ear – hell, go for it, sew it up! it's been long enough + I love earrings

hair – let it grow – no peer pressure if it looks to much body hold out long as possible w/out it looking ratty then head over to Grazia's. But remember YOU'RE the customer – get what you want! 1 length long wavy perm c/g blonde?

That's just the outside, the least important really. What's most fun about 17 is freedom

www.ingramcontent.com/pod-product-compliance
Lightning Source LLC
Chambersburg PA
CBHW071408080526
44587CB00017B/3212